by Erin Matthews

illustrated by Bridget Starr Taylor

We go on a trip.

What can we see?

We go up.
What can we see?

We can see a cloud.

We look out.
What can we see?

We can see a bird.

We look down.
What can we see?

We can see a farm.

We go very far.

Our trip was fun!

Respond to Reading

Retell

Use your own words to retell details in *What Can We See?*

Detail	Detail	Detail

Text Evidence

1. Look at page 5. What details tell you what Cat and Mouse see first? Key Details

2. Look at page 9. Where are Cat and Mouse now? Key Details

3. How can you tell that *What Can We See?* is a fantasy? Genre

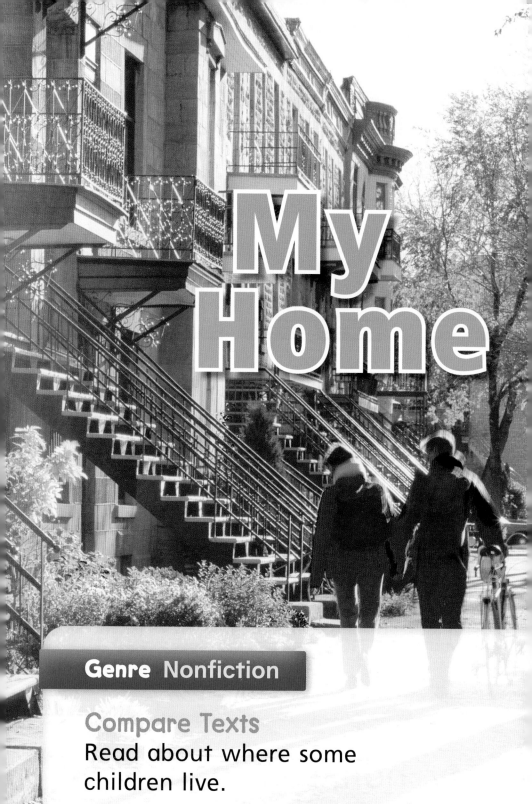

My Home

Genre Nonfiction

Compare Texts
Read about where some
children live.

My home is in a city.

My home is in a town.

My home is on a farm.

Make Connections

Do Cat and Mouse see any of the things in *My Home*? Text to Text

Focus on
Social Studies

Purpose To share pictures of places we live

What to Do

Step 1 Draw a picture of your home.

Step 2 Draw a picture of the street where you live.

Step 3 Label your pictures. Share them with the class.